my friend is struggling with . . .

Unplanned Pregnancy

Josh McDowell
& Ed Stewart

WORD PUBLISHING
NASHVILLE
A Thomas Nelson Company

Scripture quotations used in this book are from the Holy Bible, New International Version. Copyright © 1973, 1978, 1984, International Bible Society. Used by permission of Zondervan Bible Publishers.

Library of Congress Cataloging-in-Publication Data

McDowell, Josh.
    My friend is struggling with—unplanned pregnancy / by Josh McDowell and Ed Stewart.
        p. cm. — (Project 911 collection)
    Summary: Uses the story of a pregnant high school senior to deal with issues related to teen pregnancy from a Christian perspective.
    ISBN 0-8499-3796-5
    1. Teenage mothers—Juvenile literature.   2. Pregnancy, Unwanted—Juvenile literature.   3. Teenage pregnancy—Juvenile literature.   4. Teenage mothers—Religious life—Juvenile literature. [1. Pregnancy. 2. Christian life.] I. Stewart, Ed. II. Title. III. Series.
    HQ759.4 .M378 2000
    306.874'3—dc21
                                                                00-028111
                                                                CIP

Printed in the United States of America

00 01 02 03 04 05 QDT 9 8 7 6 5 4 3 2 1

Acknowledgments

We would like to thank the following people:

David Ferguson, director of Intimate Life Ministries of Austin, Texas, has made a tremendous contribution to this collection. David's influence, along with the principles of the Intimate Life message, is felt throughout each book in this collection. David has modeled before us how to be God's comfort, support, and encouragement to others. We encourage you to take advantage of the seminars and resources that Intimate Life Ministries offers. (See pages 49–54 for more information about how this ministry can serve you.)

Dave Bellis, my (Josh) associate of twenty-three years, who labored with us to mold and

acknowledgments

shape each book in this collection. Each fictional story in all eight books of the PROJECT 911 collection was derived from the dramatic audio segments of the "Youth in Crisis Resource," which Dave personally wrote. He was also responsible for the design and coordination of the entire PROJECT 911 family of resources (see pages 55–58). We are so very grateful for Dave's talents and involvement.

Joey Paul of Word Publishing not only believed in this entire project, but also consistently championed it throughout Word.

JOSH MCDOWELL
ED STEWART

Stephanie's Story

Stephanie peeked through the venetian blinds, watching her mother's car pull away until it disappeared around the corner. Then she kept her eyes glued on the empty street in front of the house for several seconds to make sure the car didn't come back.

"Stephanie, you should see yourself," Kate said with a little laugh. "You look like some kind of spy." Stephanie Cooper and Kate Holmes, both seventeen, had been best friends since fourth grade. They met because their older brothers had been best friends in high school. Summer vacation was nearly over for the two girls. The senior year they had anticipated so long together would start in two weeks.

"Mom sometimes forgets things and has to come back," Stephanie said, still watching the street. Her mother, a grocery checker, worked the late shift today—4:30 until midnight. Stephanie wanted to make sure she was gone for the evening because she didn't want to be interrupted.

"Would you rather catch a movie first and go for pizza later?" Kate asked. She was sitting cross-legged on the living-room floor studying the entertainment section of the newspaper. "We can get into the theater for half price before six."

Convinced that her mother was gone, Stephanie finally turned away from the window to face her friend. She released a long sigh. "I don't want to go out tonight."

Kate looked up from the paper, surprised. "You told me last night you wanted to do pizza and a movie tonight."

Stephanie sat down on the floor with her friend. "I know, but that was last night."

"Do you still have a touch of the flu?"

Stephanie dropped her head. "No, I don't have the flu."

"Well then . . . what?" Kate waited for an explanation.

Stephanie picked at her fingernails. "We have to talk," she said, avoiding eye contact.

Those four words were among the most serious spoken between the two friends. Both knew that the topic to follow was important. They had used the phrase only a few times during their seven years of friendship. Stephanie had used it once because a cute boy had turned her close relationship with Kate into a fierce rivalry. After they'd talked, they decided no boy was worth jeopardizing their friendship. And when Kate had said, "We have to talk," during their sophomore year, it was to announce that she had trusted Christ as her Savior through the ministry of her youth group at church. Stephanie was so impressed with the change in her friend that she began attending church with her and trusted Christ two months later. As sisters in Christ, their friendship had grown even stronger.

Stephanie felt Kate's eyes boring into the top of her head. "What's wrong, Steph?" she asked, totally serious.

3

Stephanie didn't want to answer. She had spent nearly three months trying to convince herself that there was nothing wrong. Up until two hours ago, she almost believed it.

"What's going on, Stephanie?" Kate probed with loving sisterly insistence. She leaned forward and touched her friend on the knee. "You know you have to tell me. Whatever it is, you know it's okay."

A tide of despair mixed with panic rolled up Stephanie's throat. When she finally looked up, her chin was trembling and tears flooded her eyes. "Kate, I'm pregnant." Then the dam burst and Stephanie could say no more. Burying her face in her hands, she sobbed in anguish.

"Stephanie, no!" Kate shrieked in disbelief. She rolled up on her knees and gripped her friend by the shoulders. For a full minute, Stephanie cried hard, and Kate just held her and let her own tears flow.

As the crying subsided, Kate was in Stephanie's face. "What happened? Did you miss a period? Some girls miss periods and they're not pregnant, Steph. Maybe it's something else. You can't be sure."

It was another half minute before Stephanie could respond. Wiping her eyes and nose with tissues Kate provided, she said, "I'm sure. I went to the doctor today—a clinic across town. I already missed two periods. The flu I told you about—that I told myself was the flu—was morning sickness. I'm almost three months pregnant, Kate. I . . . I. . . ." Another wave of tears choked off her words.

"Oh, Stephanie," Kate whimpered, tearing up again. She enveloped Stephanie in her arms and cried with her, repeating softly, "It's okay. I'm here. We'll get through this together."

After a couple of minutes, they were again facing each other, seated on the floor. Kate continued to hold Stephanie's hand. "What about your mom?" Kate said, dabbing her eyes.

Stephanie slowly shook her head. "She doesn't know. Nobody knows except me and you—and the doctor at the clinic."

Another minute passed in silence, except for an occasional sniffle. Stephanie drank in the comfort of her friend being there for her. She appreciated the fact that Kate was not bugging her with the inevitable questions: who, when, and how? But she realized that Kate deserved to know the answers.

Stephanie spoke softly. "Remember when Mom and I flew to the West Coast for my grandmother's funeral the first of June?"

"Yes. You were gone a whole week."

Stephanie nodded. "Well, there's this guy back there—Brent. As a kid, I saw him every summer when we went to my dad's parents for vacation. We played together and had crushes on each other—just kid stuff, that's all, because we were just little kids. After Dad and Mom divorced four years ago, I stopped going back there in the summer. I never thought about Brent again.

"Seeing him in June, I couldn't believe it. He was so different, so grown up. When I wasn't with my family, I was with Brent. We had so much fun, and by the end of the week I was spending most of my time with him. The old childish attraction came back, except we weren't kids anymore. One thing led to another, and on Friday night we . . . didn't stop.

"The whole week was unreal, like being in a movie or something. I kept telling myself that what I did back there didn't count. I came home wishing I hadn't done it and trying to brush the whole thing out of my mind. I didn't tell you anything because I guess I didn't want to admit there was anything to tell. Then I missed a period and started feeling sick in the morning. When I missed my second period, I knew I had to find out for sure. I put it off until today. I might have been able to keep denying it, except the test proves I'm pregnant."

The girls were silent for several seconds. Finally, Kate said, "Do you think you should tell Brent?"

Stephanie looked away, misty-eyed. "I don't know what to think, Kate," she said, sighing heavily. "My whole life changed two hours ago. I'm so embarrassed and ashamed. I feel so dirty. All the plans we had for our senior year. . . . " Her words trailed off to a sad whimper. "I don't know what to do."

Kate straightened up. "I know somebody who can help. We need to go see Jenny." Jenny Shaw and her husband, Doug, were volunteer youth leaders at the church Kate and Stephanie attended. Jenny had discipled each girl individually for several weeks after they trusted Christ.

"I can't tell Jenny about this," Stephanie objected. "I can hardly bear the thought of telling my mom. I don't want anybody at church to know. I just want to . . . go away."

Kate's face registered shock. "You don't mean to the West Coast, do you?"

Stephanie felt lost. After several seconds she said, "I don't know, Kate. I'm not in love with Brent, but maybe some day I could be. I don't know what to do about telling my mom. And I don't know what to do about this baby. I just want to run away and hide."

"I love you, Stephanie, and I can't let you do that," Kate said firmly. "We will get through this like we get through everything else: together. But we can't do it alone. We need to call Jenny. She'll know what to do, and she won't blab to anyone."

Stephanie knew her friend was right, but she felt so embarrassed. "Maybe Jenny won't have time to talk to us," she argued feebly.

That was all the permission Kate needed. Reaching for the phone book, she said, "We won't know until we ask." Doug and Jenny Shaw owned and operated a quick-print shop downtown. Kate looked up the number and tapped it into the phone.

"Kate, I—"

"Trust me, Steph," Kate interrupted. "I won't do anything to embarrass you." Then Jenny Shaw came on the line. As Stephanie listened, Kate arranged for the three of them to get together later that night. Jenny's husband, Doug, was leaving for the church men's retreat at 6:00. Kate and Stephanie would pick up a pizza and take it to Jenny's house by 6:30 for an evening of "girl talk" and a sleepover. Kate mentioned nothing about the shocking news.

Two hours later, Stephanie reluctantly followed Kate up to Jenny's door. They were loaded down with sleeping bags, overnight bags, and a large five-topping boxed pizza. Jenny Shaw's cheery welcome and sisterly hug boosted Stephanie's spirits. "I'm so glad you called," Jenny said. "With Doug gone for the weekend, I needed company tonight."

Stephanie tried to hide the dark tide of

despair that had been rising steadily inside her since the clinic visit. But as they sat down around the pizza box, Jenny eyed the sad face across the table and asked, "Is everything okay with you?"

Stephanie lost it again. During a torrent of tears, Stephanie's story of pregnancy tumbled out while the pizza got cold in the box. Jenny and Kate moved over beside Stephanie. "It's OK, Stephanie," they said, crying with her, "let it all out." The hesitancy Stephanie had felt about telling Jenny quickly melted in the warmth of her comforting embrace and sympathetic tears.

"My life is ruined," Stephanie moaned sadly. "I don't know if I can finish high school, let alone go to college."

"I know it hurts a lot right now," Jenny consoled. "I'm so sorry."

"And I'm so ashamed. How can I face my friends at school? And how can I tell them I'm a Christian after what I've done?"

Jenny rubbed her back gently. "I'm so sorry for you, Stephanie. But Kate and I are here for you."

"Worst of all, I have committed a terrible

sin," Stephanie said in a quavering voice. "Premarital sex is against the Bible. It's something I promised God I would never do. I know He is disappointed with me. And Kate and I committed that we would both be virgins when we married. I failed God and my best friend. I feel so worthless."

After a few minutes, Jenny suggested that they spend some time praying together. She encouraged Stephanie to bring her feelings and guilt to God while she and Kate prayed with her silently.

As they all held hands, Stephanie prayed, "God, You know what I'm feeling before I even tell You, but I need to say that I'm feeling so ashamed right now. I wish I could turn back the clock and change what I did. But I can't. I also wish these awful feelings would go away, but I can't stop feeling them."

Jenny prayed next. "Dear Lord, I hurt for Stephanie right now. There's no way I can really know what she's going through, but it hurts to see her feeling so much pain. You can look into her heart and see the pain. Help her to know that

You haven't stopped loving her, that You are willing to carry her sorrow and ease her pain."

Kate added a prayer for God to comfort her friend. Then Stephanie prayed again. "God, I have sinned. I realize that I have disobeyed You and hurt You. My pregnancy is a result of my disobedience. It's hard to accept, but I also know that You love me. You sent Your Son to die for my sins. So I ask You to forgive me right now and take control of my life from this moment on."

After several more minutes of prayer and comforting words, Jenny said, "You know you have some decisions to make, Stephanie." Stephanie nodded. "But I don't think tonight is the best time. We're all pretty emotionally drained. I suggest that we eat dinner, watch a video or two, and just be together. Tomorrow morning after breakfast we can start talking about these decisions. Would that be okay with both of you?"

Stephanie agreed quickly. "My brain is frazzled. I can't even think straight. Tomorrow would be much better." Kate nodded.

Then Stephanie said, "I just want to say that

you two are incredible. It means so much to me to have you here with me right now. I don't know what I would do without you."

"We love you, Steph," Kate said. "That's what friends are for."

After another round of caring embraces, Jenny said, "Now let's nuke this pizza and see how fast we can make it disappear!"

Time Out to Consider

Stephanie Cooper's problem is far from uncommon in our country. It is estimated that one million unmarried girls under the age of twenty get pregnant every year. About 85 percent of these pregnancies are not wanted. Half of them end in births, a third in abortion, and the rest in miscarriage. You may be reading this book because, like Stephanie, you are an adolescent, unmarried, and unintentionally pregnant. You may be overwhelmed by the same kinds of feelings, questions, and decisions. This book will help you work through the pain of what you have done and what lies ahead of you.

There are three important things to notice from the first part of Stephanie's story that may be helpful to you.

First, you may experience a wide range of emotions about being unintentionally pregnant. You may feel terribly sad, depressed, hopeless, fearful, frightened, and even angry because of what happened. You may get intensely angry at the situation, at the child growing inside you, at the boy you had sex with, or even at God for allowing it to happen. You may cry as you have never cried in your life. You may feel emotionally drained and exhausted.

It is important to understand that all these feelings are normal and natural. It is the way God wired you. Your emotions are a built-in release valve to help you handle deep inner pain. It is important to recognize these common feelings and deal with them. Of course, there are both productive and unproductive ways of expressing these emotions.

Denial. Like Stephanie, you may live in denial that you are pregnant. You may put off taking a pregnancy test, talking to anyone, or seeing a doctor, even when the early signs seem obvious. You may try to ignore the facts and hope they will just go away.

Fear. Another common reaction to pregnancy is fear. You may be afraid of how your parents or boyfriend will react. You may fear the changes that will happen in your body or the pain of labor and childbirth. You may be afraid of being rejected by friends, relatives, or your church. Or your fear may be generalized to all the unknowns ahead.

Guilt. Like Stephanie, you may feel guilty about becoming pregnant. You realize you have broken God's laws concerning sexual activity before marriage. You may be so guilt-ridden at this point that you can barely focus on anything else.

Shame. Since pregnancy eventually reveals to everyone the fact that you have been sexually active, it often brings feelings of deep shame. You don't want to be known as "that kind of girl." You are embarrassed about losing your reputation as a virgin. And you fear you will be reminded of your shame for months to come as your pregnancy changes your appearance.

Regret. You may deeply wish, as Stephanie does, that you could turn back the clock and change the circumstances that resulted in your getting pregnant. Knowing that you can't change the past may leave you under a dark cloud of regret. You may feel you have ruined your life or your boyfriend's life. You may think you have shattered your parents' reputation in the church or the community. You may be feeling for the first time the pain of facing a serious consequence that cannot be undone.

How do you handle the many different and painful feelings churning within you? Jenny's and Kate's simple advice to Stephanie was sound. They encouraged her not to bottle up her feelings, but to let her pain flow out. They were there to hurt with her and to cry with her.

This response reflects Jesus' words in Matthew 5:4: "Blessed are those who mourn, for they will be comforted." Mourning is the process of getting the hurt out. You share how sad you feel so others can share your pain and hurt with you. This is God's design for blessing you and beginning to heal your inner pain. It is good and necessary that you experience the different emotions that come at this time.

A second important point from Stephanie's story involves comfort. Your greatest need as you deal with the negative emotions of what happened is for others to comfort you. That's why Jenny and Kate spent time listening to Stephanie and crying with her. In a time of deep pain, our greatest comfort comes when others hurt for us and with us. One major way God shares His comfort with us is through other people. The apostle Paul wrote, "God . . . comforts us in all our troubles, so that we can comfort those in any trouble with the comfort we ourselves have received from God" (2 Cor. 1:3, 4).

What is comfort? Maybe it will help to see first what comfort is *not.* Comfort is not a "pep talk" urging you to hang in there, tough it out, or hold it together. Comfort is not an attempt to explain why bad things happen to people. Comfort is not a bunch of positive words about God being in control and everything being okay. All of these things may be good and useful in time, but they do not fill our primary need for comfort.

People comfort us primarily by feeling our hurt and sorrowing with us. Jesus illustrated the ministry of comfort when His friend Lazarus died (see John 11). When Jesus arrived at the home of Lazarus's sisters, Mary and Martha, He wept with them (see vv. 33–35). His response is especially interesting in light of what He did next: raise Lazarus from the dead (see vv. 38–44).

Why didn't Jesus simply tell the grieving Mary and Martha, "No need to cry, My friends, because in a few minutes Lazarus will be alive again"? Because at that moment they needed someone to identify with their hurt. Jesus met Mary's and Martha's need for comfort by sharing in their sorrow and tears. Later He performed the miracle that turned their sorrow to joy.

We receive comfort when we know we are not suffering alone. Paul instructed us, "Rejoice with those who rejoice; mourn with those who mourn" (Rom. 12:15). When you experience sorrow, people may try to comfort you by cheering you up, urging you to be strong, or trying to explain away the tragic event. These people no doubt care about you and mean well by their words. But they may not know what comfort sounds like. Hopefully, there will also be someone around like Kate Holmes or Jenny Shaw who will provide the comfort you need. You will sense God's care and concern for you as this someone hurts with you, sorrows with you, and weeps with you. Kate and Jenny are good examples of what real comfort looks like in a painful and sorrowful circumstance.

Third, Stephanie dealt with the issue of her sin against God, and so must you. Premarital sex is not an unforgivable sin. As disruptive and damaging as your sin may be, not only to you, but also to your boyfriend, your families, and others, repentance is appropriate and God's forgiveness is available. First John 1:9 applies to any sin we commit, no matter how large it may seem to us: "If we confess our sins, he is faithful and just and will forgive us our sins and purify us from all unrighteousness." Those who care for you and comfort you at this time will be glad to pray with you as you confess your sin and receive God's forgiveness.

Dealing with your many feelings, welcoming the comfort of others, confessing your sin, and receiving God's forgiveness are important first steps in responding to your unintentional pregnancy. But as Jenny reminded Stephanie, there are other questions that must be considered. These questions relate to several other persons close to you whose lives will be affected by the baby growing inside you.

Stephanie's Story

Stephanie slept better than she had expected to. She woke up only a couple of times in the night after bad dreams. But she went right back to sleep both times. Just being with Kate and Jenny and allowing them to share in her pain seemed to lift some of the weight from her.

After a breakfast of homemade waffles and fresh fruit, Jenny, Stephanie, and Kate moved into the family room with cups of hot tea. It was a conversation Stephanie wished she could avoid.

"It's very important that you tell your mother about your pregnancy right away, Stephanie," Jenny began.

Stephanie winced. "I know, but she will be

really disappointed. It's been so hard on her since Dad left. I hate to add another burden to her life."

"Would you like me to go with you when you tell her?" Jenny offered.

Stephanie released a sigh of relief. "I was hoping you would. Thanks."

"Is your mom home today? Can we talk to her later?" Jenny pressed.

"Yes, she's off today," Stephanie said, fidgeting nervously. "We can tell her today, I guess. But what do I say?"

"We'll talk about that soon," Jenny assured her, "after you have a better idea what you're going to do. What about your father? I don't believe I know him."

Stephanie shook her head. "Dad left Mom four years ago. He lives out of state. We don't hear from him much. I also have an older brother at the university."

Jenny nodded. "You and your mother will know best how to tell them your news." After a brief pause to gather her thoughts, Jenny said, "Now I want to ask you several questions on some topics you are probably already thinking about. You don't have to make these decisions today. But it's important that you have an idea what you're going to do before we talk to your mother."

"All right."

Jenny's tone was serious. "First, are you in any way considering an abortion?"

The question did not take Stephanie by surprise. "If you had asked me that question six months ago, I would have said, 'No way, never in a million years.' Even before I became a Christian I was dead-set against abortion. But I wasn't pregnant then. Now I realize why so many girls get abortions. On the surface it seems like the easy answer to all my problems. It's scary how attractive abortion has appeared to me, especially in the last month."

Kate sounded alarmed. "Stephanie, you're not really thinking—"

"No, not at all," Stephanie cut in firmly. "I know abortion is wrong. I'm not going to make my mistake worse by disobeying God again. Besides, there is a living person inside me, and I am committed to loving both God and people.

Abortion would not be the loving way to treat this person."

"I admire your commitment to loving and obeying God, Stephanie," Jenny said, "even though it's not the easy way out."

"Me too," Kate chimed in.

"But I would like you to make me a promise, Stephanie," Jenny added. "You may be pressured by Brent or his family or some of your relatives and friends to get an abortion. If you are ever tempted to take the easy way out, I want you to call me—any time, night or day. Will you promise to do that?"

"Yes, I will," Stephanie answered with conviction. "Thanks for being willing to hold me accountable."

Jenny moved on to her next question. "Do you love Brent? Do you want to marry him?"

Stephanie frowned. "I don't think I love Brent at all. I hardly know him. Our relationship was childish and selfish I suppose—nothing to build a marriage on. Besides, he lives out west and I live here. We don't have anything in common . . . except this." She touched her abdomen, which was beginning to make room for the fetus within.

"Would you consider raising the child yourself as a single parent?" Jenny said.

"I don't know," Stephanie said, searching the ceiling in thought. "I've always wanted to be a mother, and there are many things about having a child that appeal to me. But I haven't even finished high school yet. I don't have a job, and it's not fair to ask Mom to support us both. I also wonder if being raised by a working mom is really the best thing for my child. I need to think about this more."

Jenny continued, "How would you feel about Brent or his parents raising your child, if they wanted to do so?"

Stephanie frowned again. "I don't even know his parents. If I gave the child up, I would want to make sure it would go to an excellent home."

"So you've already thought about adoption?" Kate interjected.

After a sigh, Stephanie said, "I know that it's an option, but I need to learn more about it. And whatever I decide, I think Brent should have a vote."

"Then you're sure Brent is the father?" Jenny said.

Stephanie forced a humorless laugh. "The only time in my life I have sex—unprotected or otherwise—and I get pregnant. Yes, Brent is definitely the father."

Stephanie, Jenny, and Kate spent another hour talking through the many choices Stephanie would have to make regarding her baby's future. Kate and Jenny promised to be available to help her in any way they could: take her to medical appointments, make arrangements for finishing school after the baby comes, talk to adoption agencies if she chose to let someone else raise the baby.

Then Jenny helped Stephanie think through what she would say when they sat down with her mother later in the day to break the news. Finally, they joined hands in prayer again. Kate and Jenny asked God to fill Stephanie with His wisdom and perseverance through the months ahead and to help her with the immediate tasks of talking to her mother, father, brother, and Brent and his family.

Stephanie wished she could stay in the warm, supportive environment she had found at Jenny's house. But she knew what she had to do next. Kate had to go home and get ready for her Saturday afternoon job of cleaning offices with her brother. She promised to be praying for Stephanie. As she drove away, Stephanie got into Jenny's car, and they headed for the meeting with Stephanie's mother.

Time Out to Consider

Stephanie needed more than the comfort of her mentor and friend to get her through the emotional upheaval of discovering she was pregnant, and so do you. There are two more important elements that hopefully are being supplied to you.

First, you need the support of others. What's the difference between comfort and support? People supply the comfort you need when they share your sorrow emotionally. People supply the support you need by helping you during this time in practical, helpful ways. The day-to-day tasks of life go on even during difficult circumstances. But you may have little attention or energy for such things because you are dealing with a heavy emotional burden. You need temporary help just to get these things done. You need the help of people who are committed to obeying Galatians 6:2: "Carry each other's burdens, and in this way you will fulfill the law of Christ."

Think about the ways Stephanie was supported by Jenny and Kate. They helped her talk through the critical questions and decisions facing her. They offered to provide transportation when needed. They promised to help Stephanie through the difficulties of finishing her senior year during pregnancy and childbirth. They offered to assist her through the adoption process if she opted to give up her baby. Jenny and Kate assured Stephanie that they would be there to meet her practical needs as well as her emotional needs.

You may be tempted to ignore or to refuse the support offered by others. You may feel that you can handle everything yourself, or you may not want others to be bothered with things you normally do for yourself. Resist that temptation.

God put Galatians 6:2 in the Bible because He knows there are times we should rely on the support of others. This is such a time. Let other people do things for you, and be grateful for their help. It is one of the ways God is providing for your needs at this time.

What if you have a need and nobody steps up to offer help? Ask for it. There is nothing wrong with telling a trusted friend, a youth leader, or your minister about your need and asking for help. In most cases, people are more than willing to help out; they just don't know what needs to be done. Feel free to help people support you at this time by letting them know what you need.

Second, you need the encouragement of others. You receive encouragement when someone does something thoughtful to lift your spirits. Stephanie was encouraged by the devotion of her friends to meet with her and pray with her. In the weeks and months to come, she will receive encouragement every time one of them called to see how she was doing, sent a card or note, shared an uplifting Scripture verse, or gave her an understanding hug. Encouraging deeds like these may not seem as practical as providing transportation or running errands, but they are just as necessary.

Once again, if you do not receive the encouragement you need, ask for it. It's okay to tell someone who cares about you, "I need a hug" or "I just need you to be with me for a while."

In the midst of receiving comfort, support, and encouragement from two people who love her, Stephanie had some questions to answer. Not only did she need to make some decisions about her own life, but she also had the life of her unborn infant to consider. The following questions may not be pleasant to think about or easy to answer. But they will start you on the track to dealing with the issues that accompany your pregnancy. Consider going through these questions with someone like Jenny Shaw or Kate Holmes: a youth leader, trusted friend, parent, or minister.

Are you certain you are pregnant? Have you missed a period? Have you taken an in-home pregnancy test? Have you been examined by a doctor? If you have not confirmed your suspicions of pregnancy, do so. If you need help with this step, ask a mature Christian friend or leader.

Who knows about your pregnancy? As Jenny urged Stephanie, it is very important that you immediately disclose your condition to your parents and to your boyfriend and his family. Suggestions for a meeting with your parents are found later in this booklet. Beyond the close circle of the involved families, you need inform others only if and when you choose.

Are you considering an abortion? Abortion may seem like a quick and relatively easy solution to your unintentional pregnancy. Before you take that option, consider that you are carrying in your womb a living person. God can see the developing form of that individual already (see Ps. 139:13–16), and He already knows that baby just as He has known you from the time you were in your mother's womb (see Jer. 1:5). Your baby's heart is likely beating already, and soon you will be able to feel him or her turn and kick inside you. This person will continue to develop until the time of childbirth, then the newborn will eventually grow into a child, an adolescent, and finally a mature adult. That small life within you may only be at the beginning stages of growth, but it is already a person. Abortion ends the life of this person.

An abortion is a horrible means of terminating a human life. Most abortions are done by suction aspiration. A vacuum tube is inserted into the uterus and the powerful suction removes the child in broken and torn pieces. Another method is dilation and curettage (D and C), in which a loop-shaped knife slices and scrapes the baby from the womb. Yet another procedure is a saline injection through the mother's abdomen into the baby's sac. The solution gradually and violently poisons the baby, then the mother goes into labor and delivers a tiny dead body.

Many pregnant women who submit to abortion suffer mental and emotional torment for years when they realize what they have done to their babies. Abortion is the act of killing the person who will one day call you Mommy. You may be overwhelmed right now by the other complications of your unplanned pregnancy. But there are better ways to respond to your situation than to end the life of the innocent person who was conceived through your mistake.

Are you considering marriage? You should consider marriage to the child's father only if there are sound reasons beyond seeking to "legalize" your pregnancy. If you can answer most of the questions below in the positive, perhaps you should discuss this option with those giving you support and counsel.

- Do you and the father of your child want to be married now? Were you planning to be married before you discovered you were pregnant?

- Are you and the father of your child mature enough mentally, emotionally, and spiritually to take on the responsibilities of husband and wife, father and mother?

- If you marry now, what consequences will it have on the schooling and future careers of you and the father? Will you be able to provide financially for the child?

- Do close family members and trusted adult friends agree that marriage is the best thing for you, the father, and the child?

- Do you have supportive family and friends who are willing to help you if you decide to marry and parent the child with the father?

Are you considering single parenthood? Use the questions below to help you evaluate the option of parenting your child alone for now.

- If you choose single parenthood, what consequences will it have on your education and future career? How will this option affect your child?

- Where will you live, and how will you financially support your child?

- Who will care for your child while you work or go to school? Do you consider the idea of child care by others ideal, acceptable, or unacceptable?

- If you raise your child without his or her natural father, do you know someone (such as your father, your adult brother, an adult male friend, etc.) who is willing to serve as a positive, Christian male role model for your child?

- Are you mature enough mentally, emotionally, and spiritually to parent a child alone? Can you provide adequate care for the child's emotional, physical, and spiritual development?

- Do you have supportive family and friends who are willing to help you if you decide to parent the child alone?

Are you considering adoption? If you choose adoption, your child will be raised by someone else. Some adoptions are considered "open," where you meet the adoptive parents and maintain some type of ongoing personal contact with them. Other adoptions are "closed," where you choose adoptive parents based on background information without knowing their names or where they live. Assuming that you find suitable prospective parents, will you be able to choose adoption? Consider the following questions to help you evaluate this option.

- What are the advantages for you and your child if you choose adoption? For example, one advantage may be that you will be able to finish school and pursue the career you had planned. A disadvantage may be that you will suffer considerable loss in allowing someone else to raise your child. List all the advantages and disadvantages you can think of: educational, economic, emotional, relational, spiritual.

- Considering these advantages and disadvantages, how does adoption compare with the other options available to you?

- Do close family members and trusted adult friends agree that adoption is the best option for you and the child?

You do not have to make these decisions in a matter of hours or even days. Prayerfully talk through the options with family members and trusted friends until you are confident that your decision will both honor God and secure your child's best interests.

The process usually begins by telling your parents about your pregnancy, something Stephanie is about to do.

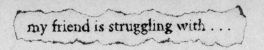

Stephanie's Story

Stephanie felt terrible about the news she was bringing to her mother. Jenny had said that her parents would probably experience many of the same emotions she was struggling through: confusion, fear, guilt, shame. They may even feel a sense of betrayal and anger over Stephanie's pregnancy. "Just like you," Jenny had said as she drove Stephanie home, "your parents need time to adjust to the news of your pregnancy and its implications on their lives." Still, Stephanie wished she did not have to burden her mother with the news.

When the two of them arrived, Stephanie's mother, Claire, was getting ready to run a few errands. "Jenny and I need to talk to you about something, Mom," Stephanie said. "Can we sit down for a few minutes?" Appearing suspicious of her daughter's serious mood and Jenny's presence, Claire agreed. They sat around a small table in the breakfast nook.

After drawing a deep breath and releasing it slowly, Stephanie said, "I found out yesterday . . . that I'm . . . pregnant."

Claire's face clouded with disbelief. "You . . . you're pregnant? Stephanie, why . . . how . . . ?"

Stephanie summarized her encounter with Brent in June and the results of the pregnancy test the previous afternoon. Her mother listened in stunned silence.

"Mom, I am so sorry to disappoint you like this," she continued as warm tears trickled down her cheeks. "I never wanted this to happen. I made a terrible mistake. With Jenny's help, I have confessed my sin to God and asked for His forgiveness. But I know what I have done will be an embarrassment and an extra burden to you. I apologize and ask you to forgive me."

Claire began to weep. "Of course I forgive you, Stephanie," she said. "I am shocked and disappointed and hurt, but I forgive you." Mother and daughter embraced, held each other, and cried together.

As Stephanie and her mother dabbed their eyes with tissues, Jenny said, "Claire, Stephanie and I have spent some time talking about the many implications of her pregnancy on her life and yours. She will need some time and your support to make all the necessary decisions. But we thought it would be good for her to share with you what she is thinking so far." Then she nodded to Stephanie.

"First, I want you to know that I will not have an abortion," she stated firmly. "It's wrong, and I won't do it."

"I'm relieved to hear you say that, honey," Claire said. "And I know God is pleased with your decision, even though it leaves you with greater responsibility for dealing with the child."

Stephanie went on. "And I'm not planning to marry Brent, at least not now. We're not in love, and we're not mature enough for marriage. I think Brent will agree. I hope you will help me talk to Brent and his family when the time comes."

"Of course I will," Claire assured her. "But what are your plans for the baby?"

Stephanie knew her answer to that question would deeply affect her mom, dad, and other family members. The baby would not only be her child, it would also be the first grandchild in the family. "I don't know yet," she answered. "I hope you will talk with me and pray with me about whether I should keep the baby or consider adoption. I know it will be the most difficult decision of my life so far. I want to take my time and be sure."

Claire nodded her agreement. "Thank you for including me. That means a lot to me."

The three of them continued to talk for almost an hour about many of the implications of Stephanie's pregnancy. She expressed her desire to at least start classes for the fall term. Jenny suggested that Claire and Stephanie discuss the issue with school officials on Monday. They debated how it would be best for Stephanie to tell her father and brother about the pregnancy, finally deciding that a phone call later in the day would be sufficient. Stephanie said she would also call Brent that evening, asking her mother to be with her when she did.

They spent a little time comparing the advantages and disadvantages of single parenthood and adoption. The discussion turned to Stephanie's goals for education and career and how these goals would be impacted by each option. Just before leaving, Jenny led a prayer for God's wisdom and guidance as Stephanie and Claire continued to sort through the options and implications of the pregnancy.

Stephanie was still awake at midnight, lying in her dark room, replaying the events of the day. There had been more tears when she talked to her father and then her brother, Joe, by telephone. Dad was disgusted and angry at the news, and Joe's "holier-than-thou" response made her feel like a tramp. Stephanie prayed that God would help her mend those relationships, which were very important to her.

Brent didn't believe the news until Stephanie gave him the phone number at the clinic, saying he could call Monday and talk to the doctor himself. Then he seemed so rattled that he didn't know what to say. Stephanie encouraged him to talk to his parents and call her in a few days.

For the last several minutes before falling asleep, Stephanie placed her hands on her tummy. She imagined what her baby looked like now and what it would look like at birth. Was it a boy or a girl? Would it look more like her or like

Brent? Would this baby have a better opportunity for a happy, fulfilling life in the home of adoptive parents, or should she take responsibility for it no matter what the cost to her? Question after question came to her, but there were no answers.

Stephanie's last thought of the day was a peaceful one. She was not alone in her difficult and painful circumstance. Thanks to her youth leader, Jenny Shaw; her best friend, Kate; and an understanding mother, she knew she was on the right track.

Time Out to Consider

It is vitally important that you sit down with your parents as soon as possible to tell them about your pregnancy and begin discussing the implications on your life and theirs. Here are several steps that will help you prepare for and carry out such a meeting.

Decide if you want someone else to go with you. Stephanie was grateful to have the counsel and encouragement of her youth leader, Jenny Shaw. Perhaps you would feel more confident about the meeting with your parents if someone went with you. If you have shared your situation with someone like Jenny—a youth leader, a mature friend, or your minister—that person may be willing to go along when you talk to your parents.

Schedule a time to meet at your parents' earliest convenience. Plan to talk to your parents as soon as possible. You don't want them to hear your news from another source. Find a time and place for your meeting that will be free from interruptions and distractions. You might say to your parents, "I have something important I want to discuss with you. When could we sit down and talk?"

Be straightforward. Get right to the point. Either you or the "Jenny Shaw" who is with you should state clearly to your parents that you are pregnant. Beating around the bush will only make your disclosure more painful for everyone.

Express your regret and repentance. Since you are their daughter, your parents will suffer many of the same experiences, emotions, and pressures you will suffer in the coming months. Are you sorry for the difficulties your mistake will put them through in the coming weeks? Express your heartfelt sorrow and regret to them in your own words, as Stephanie Cooper did to her mother.

Discuss your options with them. Express and explain your current thoughts on the issues of abortion, marriage, single parenthood, and adoption. Invite their counsel and prayers as you decide whether to raise the baby yourself (or with the father through marriage) or to give it up for adoption. Your parents may also be willing to help you share your news with other family members and with the child's father and his family. Respectfully ask for your parents' help and support in the coming months.

Close with prayer. If your parents are Christians, ask them to join you in a time of prayer. Together ask God for His direction and help in the coming months as you deal with all the activities related to pregnancy and the birth of the child.

As you convey respect for your parents' feelings and a willingness to listen to their concerns and suggestions, you increase the possibility that they will become your helpful supporters in the

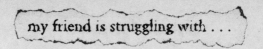

months ahead. Knowing that your dearest loved ones are on your side will help lift some of the emotional burden from your shoulders, as Stephanie discovered.

Stephanie's Story

Stephanie waited until she and Jenny were in the car to tell the latest news. Claire had to work at the market, so Jenny had volunteered to drive Stephanie to her scheduled sixth-month prenatal examination.

Placing a hand on her ballooning tummy, Stephanie announced, "It's a girl. The images were real clear this month, they said. Everything looks good. The baby is healthy and growing."

"A girl—that's wonderful," Jenny said with guarded enthusiasm. "Are you doing okay?"

"Me? Yes, I'm doing well. The doctor says I'm a couple of pounds overweight, but she wasn't worried about it."

"I mean are you okay emotionally, knowing that the baby is a girl?" Jenny pressed. "Does it make you want to change your mind?"

Stephanie thought about it for a moment. "I had a hunch that it was a girl, so I'm pleased about that. There is still a part of me that would love to take care of my little girl. But Mom and I prayed about this a lot, talked a lot, and cried a lot. I'm convinced that the best thing for the baby is to grow up with a mother and father who love her and can take care of her. We are going ahead with our plans to share her with a loving family."

"And Brent and his parents feel okay about that?" Jenny said.

"Yes. It might be different if the father were someone I was already planning to marry. But Brent and I are not going to be together, we both know that. And it might be different if I was mature enough to raise the child by myself, but I'm not. His family and mine agree that the baby deserves a better home than either Brent or I can provide."

Jenny drove in silence for a minute. "I really admire you, Stephanie, for putting the baby's welfare above your own desires."

The affirmation warmed Stephanie's heart. "Thanks, but I couldn't have done it without people like you and Mom and Kate. Your support and encouragement have made our decision easier."

Jenny nodded her appreciation for the comment. Then she said, "How is school going?"

"Very well. I plan to stay in class almost until my due date. Then I'll homeschool until the baby comes. I should be back in school a couple of weeks after the birth, so I can graduate with my class."

"I'm really happy for you, Stephanie," Jenny said. "Everything seems to be working out."

Stephanie hummed her agreement. "Romans 8:28 has been very special to me in the last few months. God is bringing good out of my not-so-good situation and the consequences I am facing."

Jenny smiled. "That's the best news of all, Stephanie."

Time Out to Consider

Even in the difficulties surrounding your pregnancy and its implications, there is good news.

God's love for you has not changed. What

God told Israel is true about you: "I have loved you with an everlasting love" (Jer. 31:3). And what the psalmist said about God is still true today: "Give thanks to the LORD, for he is good; his love endures forever" (Ps. 107:1). God loves you as much today as He did before you became pregnant.

God will use your not-so-good situation for good. Romans 8:28 was a source of encouragement to Stephanie, and it can be for you: "We know that in all things God works for the good of those who love him, who have been called according to his purpose." God did not cause your situation, but He is all-loving and all-powerful, and He can bring good out of it for you, your baby, and your family (see Gen. 50:20).

Time will help heal your pain. The sorrow and discouragement you may feel right now will not last. As bad as your situation may seem to you, it will become easier to handle with every passing day. Psalm 30:5 promises, "Weeping may remain for a night, but rejoicing comes in the morning." Someday—perhaps not soon, but eventually—the hurt will pass.

You can begin the healing process right now by turning to God in prayer and seeking His comfort. Use these "prayer-starters" to help you express your thoughts and feelings to God:

God, Your Word says that You heal the broken-hearted and bind up their wounds, and I need that right now. I'm feeling like . . .

And the Bible also says that You comfort us in all our troubles, so I need to ask You to comfort me by . . .

Finally, God, Your Word says that I should cast all my anxiety on You, because You care for me. I don't know if I can do that, but I'm willing to try. I have so many things on my mind and so many problems and worries. Help me to throw them all onto You, to let You take care of them, to let You carry the burden and to trust You to work things out better than I could. Help me, please, in the name of Jesus, who loved me enough to die for me. Amen.

APPENDIX

Several times in this book I have mentioned the
work of Dr. David Ferguson. David's ministry
has had such a profound effect on me in the past
several years that I want you to have every opportunity to be exposed to his work and ministry.
David and his wife, Teresa, direct a ministry
called Intimate Life Ministries.

Who and What Is Intimate Life Ministries?
Intimate Life Ministries (ILM) is a training and
resource ministry whose purpose is to *assist in
the development of Great Commandment ministries worldwide*. Great Commandment ministries—ministries that help us love God and our
neighbors—are ongoing ministries that deepen

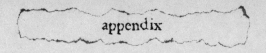

our intimacy with God and with others in marriage, family, and the church.

Intimate Life Ministries comprises:

- A network of **churches** seeking to fortify homes and communities with God's love;

- A network of **pastors and other ministry leaders** walking intimately with God and their families and seeking to live vulnerably before their people;

- A team of **accredited trainers** committed to helping churches establish ongoing Great Commandment ministries;

- A team of **professional associates** from ministry and other professional Christian backgrounds, assisting with research, training, and resource development;

- **Christian broadcasters, publishers, media, and other affiliates,** cooperating to see marriages and families reclaimed as divine relationships;

- **Headquarters staff** providing strategic planning, coordination, and support.

HOW CAN INTIMATE LIFE MINISTRIES SERVE YOU?
ILM's Intimate Life Network of Churches is an effective, ongoing support and equipping relationship with churches and Christian leaders. There are at least four ways ILM can serve you:

1. *Ministering to Ministry Leaders*
ILM offers a unique two-day "Galatians 6:6" retreat to ministers and their spouses for personal renewal and for reestablishing and affirming ministry and family priorities. The conference accommodations and meals are provided as a gift to ministry leaders by cosponsoring partners. Thirty to forty such retreats are held throughout the U.S. and Europe each year.

2. *Partnering with Denominations and*
   Other Ministries
Numerous denominations and ministries have partnered with ILM by "commissioning" them to equip their ministry leaders through the Galatians

6:6 retreats along with strategic training and ongoing resources. This unique partnership enables a denomination to use the expertise of ILM trainers and resources to perpetuate a movement of Great Commandment ministry at the local level. ILM also provides a crisis-support setting to which denominations may send ministers, couples, or families who are struggling in their relationships.

3. *Identifying, Training, and Equipping Lay Leaders*
ILM is committed to helping the church equip its lay leaders through:

- *Sermon Series* on several Great Commandment topics to help pastors communicate a vision for Great Commandment health as well as identify and cultivate a core lay leadership group.

- *Community Training Classes* that provide weekly or weekend training to church staff and lay leaders. Classes are delivered by Intimate

Life trainers along with ILM video-assisted training, workbooks, and study courses.

- *One-Day Training Conferences* on implementing Great Commandment ministry in the local church through marriage, parenting, or singles ministry. Conducted by Intimate Life trainers, these conferences are a great way to jump-start Great Commandment ministry in a local church.

4. *Providing Advanced Training and Crisis Support*

ILM conducts advanced training for both ministry staff and lay leaders through the Leadership Institute, focusing on relational ministry (marriage, parenting, families, singles, men, women, blended families, and counseling). The Enrichment Center provides support to relationships in crisis through Intensive Retreats for couples, families, and singles.

For more information on how you, your church, or your denomination can take advantage of the many services and resources, such as

the Great Commandment Ministry Training
Resource offered by Intimate Life Ministries,
write or call:

Intimate Life Ministries
P.O. Box 201808
Austin, TX 78720-1808
1-800-881-8008
www.ilmministries.com

For Adults & Groups

This watershed book is for parents, pastors, youth workers, or anyone interested in seeing youth not only survive but thrive in today's culture.

Book on Audio

This book, directed specifically to fathers, offers ten qualities to form deepened relationships between dads and their kids.

Begin your church-wide emphasis with an adult group experience using this five-part video series. Josh provides biblical insights for relationally connecting with your youth.

Experience the Connection

ABOUT THE AUTHORS

JOSH MCDOWELL, internationally known speaker, author, and traveling representative of Campus Crusade for Christ, International, has authored or coauthored more than fifty books, including *Right from Wrong*, and *Josh McDowell's Handbook on Counseling Youth*. Josh and his wife, Dottie, have four children and live in Dallas, Texas.

ED STEWART is the author or coauthor of numerous Christian books. A veteran writer, Ed Stewart began writing fiction for youth as a coauthor with Josh McDowell. He has since authored four suspense novels for adults. Ed and his wife, Carol, live in Hillsboro, Oregon. They have two grown children and four grandchildren.